Chain Mail +Color

20 jewelry projects using aluminum
jump rings, scales, and disks

Vanessa
Walilko

KALMBACH BOOKS

WAUKESHA, WI

Kalmbach Books
21027 Crossroads Circle
Waukesha, Wisconsin 53186
www.Kalmbach.com/Books

Published in 2015
19 18 17 16 15   1 2 3 4 5

Manufactured in the United States of America

ISBN: 978-1-62700-123-6
EISBN: 978-1-62700-129-8

Editor: Erica Swanson
Book Design: Carole Ross
Photographer: William Zuback, James Forbes

Library of Congress Control Number: 2014950476

Contents

Introduction

I signed up for my first chain mail class in 2006.

Initially I took the class just to get access to the metalsmithing studio at a local arts center, but I quickly fell in love with the craft. The rhythmic pattern of the chain mail weaves was soothing and meditative for me. I'd been making jewelry since I was eight, working with tiny seed beads to make jewelry, sculptures, and wearable art—and chain mail offered me a new medium for creative expression. Not long after learning some basic weaves, I started putting together chain mail clothing.

I never expected that chain mail would be the center of my life, but it has been for the past several years. I exhibit at art fairs around the country, selling my chain mail jewelry. My wearable chain mail art pieces have been featured in competitions, exhibitions, and magazines around the world. Every day, I'm grateful (and a little bewildered) that I get to do what I love for a living.

I've also been teaching chain mail jewelry classes since 2007. Teaching chain mail is one of the most rewarding experiences of my career. I love watching new students engage with the materials to create something beautiful. It's so exciting to watch students come alive when they make something with their own hands.

I decided to write a book about working with aluminum because I love what can be done with the metal. Aluminum is incredibly lightweight. It is only one-third of the weight of more familiar metals, which makes it the perfect material for larger pieces, like clothing. Aluminum can also be anodized to produce vibrant colors, unlike other metals. Aluminum components also add a new dimension to chain mail. Because the material is so lightweight, you can add all kinds of fun shapes like scales and disks in different colors into the mix.

No matter what medium I'm working in, I'm always looking to push the boundaries of what is expected, and these pieces offer something that's never been seen before. My hope was to write a book that would make these techniques accessible to those new to the craft, and give seasoned mailers some new techniques to play with.

— *Vanessa*

Basics

ALUMINUM

Most of us are familiar with soda cans and aluminum foil. Using aluminum in jewelry, however, is a relatively new idea. All of the projects in this book are made using two types of aluminum: bright aluminum and anodized aluminum. Bright aluminum refers to a particular alloy of aluminum mixed with magnesium. (For ease in the instructions, I refer to the bright aluminum color as "silver.") The wire is then drawn through a diamond die to produce a lustrous finish with minimal gray ruboff on the skin.

Anodizing is a way of dying the surface of the aluminum. With the anodizing process, aluminum can be transformed into bright, eye-catching colors that can't be replicated with other materials.

There are many steps to anodizing aluminum. When aluminum is exposed to air, a protective layer of aluminum oxide is formed on the surface of the metal to prevent further corrosion underneath. However, this aluminum oxide also makes it impenetrable to any dye. To prepare the metal for anodizing, the first step is to immerse it in a bath of sulfuric acid and water. The acid eats away at the aluminum oxide on the surface of the metal.

Now the fun part happens: While the aluminum is in the acidic bath, an electrical current is run through the metal. This current is low—between 4 and 16 volts. The aluminum is left in the bath until it becomes porous. Since the surface is now highly susceptible to grease and dirt, a dye is added immediately and penetrates the surface of the metal. It's not a simple color coating that can chip or peel off—the color infuses the surface of the aluminum. The metal is then sealed in a variety of ways, including steam.

Working with Anodized Aluminum

Since chemicals and electricity are involved in the process of anodizing aluminum, I wouldn't recommend it if you're just getting started. If you're really interested in anodizing aluminum yourself, other books can teach you how to set up your own anodizing station at home. This book, however, will focus on using pre-anodized aluminum shapes to produce

tactile, colorful, unique jewelry. While you are encouraged to cut your own shapes from anodized aluminum sheets if you're feeling particularly ambitious, a number of pre-cut anodized aluminum shapes are available from commercial suppliers.

Remember that any anodized aluminum shapes you've purchased commercially are produced on industrial die-cutters, so the shapes may have sharp or ragged edges. These are very easy to smooth out with a metal file or sandpaper. You might also notice residue of cutting lubricant on the commercially-made pieces. This lubricant is non-toxic and washes off easily with soap and water.

List of Suppliers

Aluminumchainmail.com
- Kits for all of the projects in this book
- Anodized aluminum disks, washers, and scales

Beaducation.com
- Aluminum and anodized aluminum blanks in solid colors and patterns, as well as fun shapes like birds, hearts, leaves, and states
- Power Punch pliers and aluminum stamps

Bluebuddhaboutique.com
- Anodized aluminum rings and small scales

Candtdesigns.com
- Anodized aluminum rings, findings, and chain
- Anodized aluminum scales, both regular and treated with a UV-reactive finish, which shows up under black light

Firemountaingems.com
- Anodized aluminum jump rings, components, and bells
- Anodized aluminum wire and pre-made chain

Metaldesignz.com
- Anodized aluminum rings
- Pre-made chain, findings, and laser-engraved scales

More About
Aluminum

Aluminum is the most abundant metal on the planet, but it had limited use until the 1800s. Aluminum always appears in nature with other elements, which makes it difficult to mine. The ore has to be refined to reveal the pure metal, and the power able to accomplish this task was only available once refineries could be powered with electricity. Up until the late 1800s, aluminum was so difficult to extract from ore that it was more valuable than gold.

People have been using aluminum for more than 5,000 years for various purposes, usually in the form of "alum." Alum is a white powder that contains aluminum, along with other metals such as potassium. The ancient Babylonians used these alum salts to make dyes stick to textiles, and the ancient Greeks and Romans used alum salts to dress wounds. Aluminum oxide is also the main component of corundum, which crystallizes into rubies and sapphires.

Once aluminum could be extracted from ore, this sturdy, lightweight material began to be used in a variety of ways. Aluminum is an incredibly versatile metal that is used in vehicle parts, license plates, siding, roofing, and product packaging. For those of us who try to be eco-friendly, aluminum is a great option. Aluminum is 100% recyclable, making it an earth-conscious material. Unlike paper and other materials, aluminum doesn't break down during the recycling process. The aluminum rings and shapes you work with could have been a soda can not long ago. In fact, the recycling process for aluminum cans is so efficient, that a new can can appear on store shelves just 60 days after the cans it was made from were tossed into a bin.

Choosing Jump Rings

Anodized aluminum jump rings (referred to simply as "rings" in the instructions) are available in a wide variety of sizes. You can buy rings as thin and small as 20-gauge, ⅛" inner diameter (ID) and as large as 12-gauge, 1" ID. Depending on the supplier you choose, you can also find rings with a matte finish, or with a shiny colored coat.

● **NOTE:** **Gauge refers to the thickness of the wire or sheet metal used to make the components. The higher the gauge, the thinner the metal. ID refers to the size of the ring as measured from the inner diameter. Outer diameter (abbreviated as OD) refers to the size of the ring as measured from the outer diameter.**

Rings are either saw-cut or machine-cut. Machine-cut rings have an extra little divot of metal cut from the top of the ring of the closure. Saw-cut rings have clean edges. Most of the projects in this book are made with saw-cut rings because they allow for better closures and a more professional look, but machine-cut rings are also a great option, as they are much less expensive than saw-cut rings.

While aluminum is available in a number of different alloys, all of the silver rings in this book are made from bright aluminum. Regular aluminum can leave a gray residue on clothes and skin, especially if you're wearing it on a hot summer day. However, bright aluminum is nice and shiny and requires little upkeep.

Scales

I fell in love with the possibilities of aluminum when I started working with anodized aluminum scales to create "scale mail." Unlike many other anodized aluminum shapes on the market, the scales are slightly domed, which gives an added dimension to chain mail and makes you weave in a completely new way.

Two sizes of anodized aluminum scales are used in this book. The small scales are ⅞" long and just over ½" wide, while the large scales are almost 1½" long and ⅞" wide. All of the scales that are commercially available have been stamped with a large hole near one end. In the small scales, the hole is ³⁄₁₆" in diameter (making it easy to incorporate into any piece using ³⁄₁₆" ID rings), while the hole in the large scale is ⅜" in diameter.

Scales are typically available only in solid colors, but you can also find color-fade scales and patterned scales.

● **NOTE:** While the description of the chemical process used to treat and color aluminum might undermine what I said about anodized aluminum being an eco-friendly metal option, the process of anodizing aluminum is considered environmentally safe by the U.S. Environmental Protection Agency. The by-products of anodizing aluminum—aluminum hydroxide, aluminum sulfate, and water—can be used in the secondary stage of treatment at sewage treatment plants. If you want to make metal jewelry while also being conscientious of the impact on the ecosystem, aluminum is the metal to choose.

Washers

While a couple different sizes of anodized aluminum washers are commercially available, only one size of anodized aluminum washers are used in this book. Washers are identified by two sizes: OD and ID. The OD of the washers used in this book is ½" and the ID is ¼". While a limited number of colors are available, you can use EuroPower hole punch pliers or a ¼" diameter punch to turn any ½" diameter disk into a washer.

Disks

There are countless aluminum and anodized aluminum shapes on the market today. You can find disks in many different colors and sizes, and even disks with beautiful patterns to incorporate into your pieces. Some disks have holes in the top, while others are not pre-punched. Disks come in many gauges, but most of the disks in this book are 20 gauge.

I used four sizes in this book: 1½" (extra-large), 1" (large), ¹¹⁄₁₆" (medium), and ⅜" (small) diameters.

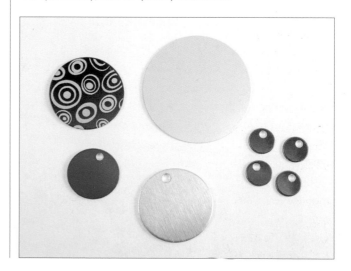

Wear and Care

I'm often asked how long anodizing lasts on aluminum shapes and rings. The answer is that it depends. Several factors go into how long the color lasts on a piece, such as the alloy used, the dye used, or whether or not the piece was sealed after anodizing. I can say this: The first pieces I made are still as colorful as they were when I first made them. The colors haven't bled from the shapes or the rings.

However, we all have different body chemistry and the pH levels of our skin will determine how we react to metals. Most people have minimal reactions to aluminum and will notice some gray rub-off on their skin if they wear an aluminum or a bright aluminum piece. Anodized aluminum rarely reacts with skin because the metal is sealed after it's anodized.

You can minimize the gray rub-off by following a few tips. If you wear moisturizer, make sure it dries completely before you put on any jewelry. I also encourage you to regularly wash your aluminum jewelry to keep dirt and oil from the surface of the metal.

Aluminum and anodized aluminum are very easy to take care of. You don't need any fancy chemicals or cleaners. You just need to apply some dish soap (with no moisturizer) to your piece and rub it under water. Rubbing all the aluminum shapes will create a good lather to remove any dirt and oil. Rinse the piece under warm water and towel dry. Basic care is all you need to keep your chain mail looking bright and new.

Is Aluminum Safe?

I often get questions from students and customers about the safety of aluminum. There is a very small percentage of the population that is allergic to aluminum. For everyone else, it's a hypoallergenic metal and a non-toxic metal. You will not absorb aluminum through your skin while working with aluminum rings and shapes, so you don't need to worry about metal toxicity.

OTHER MATERIALS

Although the majority of the pieces will be made from scales, washers, disks, and jump rings, there are a few other items that you'll need to complete the projects.

● **NOTE:**
Most projects in this book start from the clasp or the earring wire. This allows you to immediately have an anchor for your piece. You'll always know where you started your work and in which direction you need to go next.

Chain

Aluminum chain is available in a number of different sizes and colors. In my jewelry, I use two different styles of anodized aluminum chain: curb chain and cable chain. Curb chain is identified by its twisted, flattened links, while cable chain is defined by its elongated oval links. The projects in this book use two different sizes of cable chain—a small chain with 19-gauge $^3/_{32}$x$^1/_8$" links and a large chain with 14-gauge $^9/_{16}$x$^3/_8$" links—but I encourage you to play around with different styles to find what you like best.

Findings

The majority of the projects in this book are finished with toggle clasps made from lead-free pewter with rhodium, copper, or gold plating. I love toggle clasps because they're easy to put on and take off, and if you balance the weight properly on your piece, the tension will hold it firmly in place. You can substitute lobster claw clasps in any project if you prefer. I also use slide clasps for a few wider bracelets. These are made with two nesting cylinders and often feature a magnet in the end.

All of the earring wires used in the projects in this book are made from surgical steel. Some people have metal sensitivity to nickel, and all of the components used in this book are nickel-free. If you have metal allergies or sensitivities, I recommend using niobium clasps and earring wires for your projects. Even people allergic to gold can wear niobium without any skin irritation.

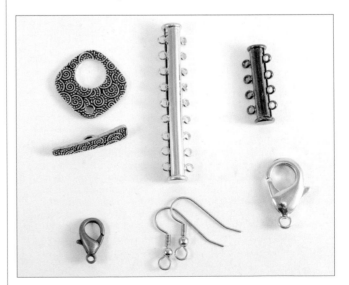

● **NOTE:**
While I would have loved to use anodized aluminum or aluminum for all of my projects, many of the clasp rings are either jewelry brass or copper. The one size of ring that I trust for the strength to hold my clasps is 18-gauge, $^1/_8$" ID, and that size simply isn't available yet in anodized aluminum.

TOOLS

Pliers

One of the things I love most about chain mail is that you have so many options for making a piece of jewelry. This can be overwhelming to someone new to the craft, so I'll give my recommendations. In my experience of making chain mail professionally and teaching classes, these are the tools that are easiest to work with.

For chain mail, I recommend using two pairs of flatnose pliers. Flatnose pliers offer the best of both worlds: The nose of the pliers is wide enough to grip the rings without slipping, and it's narrow enough to maneuver rings into tight spots. Choose a pair of pliers with a nose around ⅛" wide.

Try out different pliers to see what fits best in your hand. If you have larger hands, find pliers with longer handles so the ends of the handles don't create pressure points in the palms of your hands. You also want to make sure that the grip of the pliers is narrow or wide enough for your hands. I've found that pliers with a wide grip quickly fatigue my hands, but I can work for hours with pliers with a narrower grip. I also like lightweight pliers because it creates less strain for me, but you may prefer a heavier pair of pliers.

When choosing pliers, you also want to make sure that the pliers you buy have good springs. The strain of using pliers isn't from squeezing them closed, but pulling them apart. It's easy to grip the rings, but pulling the handles apart to open the grip is going to cause repetitive stress injuries on your hands. Find pliers that are nice and springy.

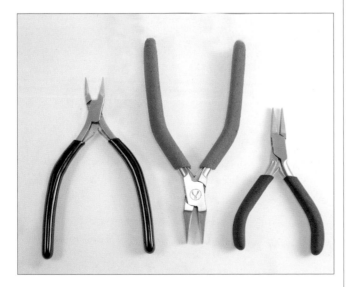

● NOTE:
Some students use bentnose or chainnose pliers for making chain mail. If you've found pliers that work for you—keep using them. If you're new to chain mail, I've found that two pairs of flatnose pliers work the best.

EuroPower Hole Punch Pliers

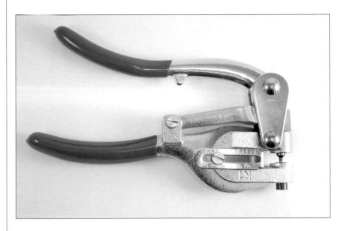

Most of the aluminum shapes you'll need for the projects in this book will already have a round hole punched near the edge, or in one corner. However, you might notice that some of the aluminum shapes that you buy are not pre-punched. I recommend using a set of EuroPower hole punch pliers.

This somewhat intimidating contraption is perfect for punching perfectly round holes in aluminum shapes. I used my pliers to punch over 4,000 holes in anodized aluminum disks to make a poncho, and they still work great!

The hole punch pliers operate by pressing interchangeable cutting dies through metal. I've punched aluminum sheet as thick as 20-gauge with these pliers easily, and they are rated for metal as thick as 16-gauge. The set comes with eight cutting dies between ³⁄₃₂–⁹⁄₃₂" in diameter, working up in ¹⁄₃₂" increments. For this book, you'll be working mostly with the ³⁄₃₂" diameter and ⅛" diameter dies.

To change dies, use the key that came with the pliers (or a flat-head screwdriver) to remove the screw between the handles. Slide out the cutting die holder to remove the die and replace it with the die you want to use. Twist the corresponding die hole from the bottom of the jaw of the hole punch pliers piece, and twist in the matching diameter hole for the die you just added.

Once the correct die is in place, start punching aluminum shapes. After working with your punch for a while (thousands of punches), you might notice the aluminum shapes sticking and then warping as you release them from the punch, but don't worry. Aluminum is sturdy and the anodizing will not come off the surface easily. If one of your pieces has bent out of shape, just flatten it between the jaws of your pliers.

If your hole punch pliers are sticking, add oil to the cutting die (extra-virgin olive oil works), and the pieces will go back to sliding off the cutting die easily.

Wire Cutters

A few projects require cutting aluminum chain. The large chain used in this book is made from unsoldered rings, so you can twist those open and closed with flatnose pliers. However, some of the thinner chain might need to be snipped. Any wire cutters will do, as long as they're strong enough to cut 18-gauge wire.

Coating Your Pliers

If you're new to chain mail, you may want to use some form of coating on your tools. When you first begin, it's easy to get a death grip on the pliers because you're learning how strongly you need to hold the pliers to open and close rings.

The easiest fix is to wrap masking tape around the jaws of your pliers tightly and cut off any excess. This is not the best option if you're planning on working with tiny rings, since it creates bulk, but when the tape wears away, you can quickly re-wrap and continue working.

Another option is to find a rubber coating solution, such as Tool Magic. This coating protects the rings from the sharp edges of the pliers. It will start to break apart after you weave a couple hundred rings (depending on the gauge or the metal you're working with), and you can peel the rest of the coating off. This option lasts longer than tape, but you have to wait several hours for the coating to dry and cure before you can work again.

I encourage you to start working without coated tools. Before making jewelry, practice opening and closing rings to develop a more sensitive feel for how much you need to grip and twist the pliers when you're making chain mail. This way, you can train yourself not to grip the rings too tightly, which will cut down on muscle fatigue in your hands and arms as you make jewelry.

TECHNIQUES

Gripping Pliers

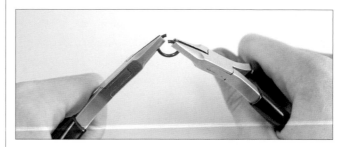

One of the most important things you can do when make chain mail is develop work habits that prevent undue stress. It takes a while not to feel awkward while holding pliers.

First, hold the pliers properly when you grip the rings. I recommend holding the pliers in the 10 and 2 position as if you were driving, with the nose of the pliers facing up. While you're doing this, make sure to keep your elbows close to your waist. The closer your arms are to your body, the more torque you can use to open and close rings. I can always tell which of my students have a history of making beadwork because they tend to keep their elbows out. This arm position works for beading, but not when you need the power to bend metal.

In this same vein, try to do as much twisting as you can from your shoulders and upper arms instead of working from your wrists. You'll run less risk of a repetitive stress injury.

● **NOTE:**
Although this technique is best for most situations, different projects call for different grips. Try out different methods of holding the pliers to see what works for you.

Opening Rings

Always twist open your jump rings. Don't pull them apart, as you'll destroy the ring's shape. If you're right-handed, twist the right side of the ring toward you. If you're left-handed, twist the left side of the ring toward you. In my years of teaching, this practice makes it easier for students to weave rings because you can weave away from yourself and always see where you're going. When you open rings toward you the opposite way, you have to either weave through the back with limited visibility or contort your arms in odd positions to weave the rings where they need to go. Chain mail should be fun—make it easy on yourself and develop the habit of opening rings toward you.

This book is written from the perspective of a right-hand dominant person. If you're left-handed or the direction of the weave seems flipped to you, turn the book upside down to view the photos. This will reverse the photos and should make the projects easier for you to follow.

Closing Rings

The basis of good chain mail is perfect closures. A perfect closure is the trickiest part of chain mail to master, and many seasoned mailers weave for years before all of their rings are closed perfectly. When you get started, you'll probably notice gaps between your rings. Don't lose hope! The more you work with rings, the more you'll get a feel for the metal and be able to close every ring well. I always tell my students that if they want to have perfect closures, they should make a piece of chain mail clothing. After closing thousands of rings with my first piece of clothing, my closures were much better than when I started.

To create jump rings, wire is coiled around a mandrel. Then, a saw cuts a chunk out of the wire to turn the coil into rings. This space between the rings needs to be overcome to make a good closure. It's not enough to simply twist the ends together; you have to work against the metal's springback.

When closing rings, you want to slightly overlap the edges of the ring and push the ends toward each other. Then draw the edges apart and overlap the edges in the opposite direction and push the ends toward each other. You should hear little clicks as the ring edges rub against each other. Draw the edges back to the center. You should barely see a gap between the edges for a good closure.

Why am I so fussy about closures? Good closures serve a practical purpose: If you close your rings properly, you never have to worry about rings or shapes accidentally falling off the piece. You also never have to worry about a gap in the ring scratching you or whoever wears your chain mail jewelry.

● **NOTE:**
At the start of each project, you'll notice a "Before You Begin" section, which lists the number of rings you should open or close before working the step-by-step instructions. It's far easier to open or close a lot of rings at once than to stop mid-project to do so.

Weaving Rings

"Weaving" a ring means to connect it to one or more rings (or aluminum shapes) in the chain mail. When weaving rings onto the piece, grip the ring in your pliers so that the end of the ring facing you is as close as possible to the pliers. This will allow you to "lead" the other end of the ring (the end facing away from you) through the other rings or shapes with

Good closures
depend on a few key components:

1. Always grip the rings flat between your pliers. If your pliers are gripping the rings at an angle, you're going to create rings that are slightly bowed.

2. Make sure that you push both ends of the rings together as you're twisting them closed with equal force. If not, you will notice that some of your rings have a little bit of an overbite, with one edge of the ring sitting slightly higher than the other. You can fix this by re-opening the ring and trying to move the edges up or down to meet each other in the center.

3. Make sure that you push the ends of the rings toward each other when they aren't facing each other. If you push metal against metal, you'll still end up with a gap between the edges of the rings.

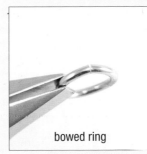
bowed ring

overlapping ring

ring with gap

ring with good closure

ease. Many new students grab the open ring from the middle when they try to weave it onto the piece and then get frustrated when it doesn't lay correctly. Many weaves require specific placements of rings, and if you don't weave rings in the correct direction, they will fall out of place or lay incorrectly. Holding the right end of the ring will ensure that you will weave all the projects in the book correctly.

THREE SIMPLE WEAVES

Chain mail is based on weaving jump rings in established patterns. For many of these projects, you can simply follow the directions on the page. For others, you will want to refer to these three common weaves.

1-in-1

A 1-in-1 chain is simple—just attach one ring at a time with no extra shapes or rings. Using smaller rings (like 18-gauge ⅛" ID) means that the chain will be sturdy and slim enough for a functional clasp that's easy to put on. For a toggle clasp

to be most effective, the chain attached to the bar part of the clasp needs to be half as long as the bar. This makes it easy to thread the bar through the ring part of the clasp.

European 4-in-1

A few projects in the book call for ribbons of European 4-in-1. This weave was used in medieval times to make armor, so it is fluid and versatile. You can use a wide range of ring sizes to make it. To make a ribbon of European 4-in-1, begin by closing twice as many rings as you open.

1. Weave an open ring through two closed rings, and close the ring. Anchor the beginning of your piece with either a length of wire or by weaving the open ring through a clasp.

2. Fan out the two rings, and flip them underneath the center ring. You'll always know that you've oriented the weave in the correct direction if the center ring sits at an angle that matches the curve of your thumb. This center ring and two hanging rings is considered a single "unit" of European 4-in-1.

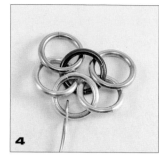

3. With a new open ring, pick up two closed rings. Weave away from you through the front of the right fanned ring, turn, and weave toward you though the back of the left fanned ring. Close the ring.

4. Again, fan out the two closed rings so that they sit underneath the center ring. These rings should also stack in the same direction as the fanned rings beneath them.

5. Repeat steps 3 and 4 for the length of your ribbon. To end a ribbon, weave an open ring through the last two fanned rings as described in step 2, but don't add any closed rings.

One of the common mistakes with European 4-in-1 is called a "gridlock." A gridlock most often occurs when you forget to make sure that the fanned rings on the edges of the ribbon all stack in the same direction. Remember: It's not enough to make sure that the center ring of the last unit on the ribbon lines up with the curve of your thumb. Each center ring must line up in the same way.

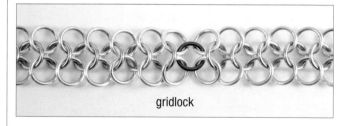

gridlock

Shaggy Shapes

Shaggy shapes is a variation of shaggy loops, a weave invented by my friend and fellow chain mail maven, Shelley Hubbs. The weave involves creating a 1-in-1 chain with two closed rings hanging off of each link in the chain. In this version, you will add aluminum shapes instead of two closed rings.

● **NOTE:**
If you want to become a chain mail pro, get used to keeping pliers in your hands as much as possible. It'll be very awkward at first, but will get easier as time goes on (I promise!). The more often you put down and pick up the piece, the easier it can be for rings to slip out of place or for you to get confused about the next step.

1. With an open ring, pick up two aluminum shapes, and close the ring. This ring and attached shapes is a single "unit" of the shaggy shapes weave.

2. Part the two shapes to open up a space between them. This is the pathway for the next ring.

3. With a new open ring, pick up two new shapes and weave through the open space. Close the ring.

4. Part the shapes to create a space for the next ring.

5. Repeat steps 3 and 4 until you reach your desired length.

When weaving, you might notice shapes bunched up on one side of the ring. This happens when you forget to split the shapes before weaving on the new ring. Just re-open the ring, position the shapes in the correct position, and close the ring.

TERMINOLOGY

Concave and Convex

Scale mail is assembled differently than other types of chain mail. You'll work on the underside of the piece, so you can better see the rings and the nature of the weave. This orientation while weaving means that the "front" of the weave is actually the "back." To avoid confusion—since the front and back of the piece are opposite of the front and back of the finished piece (and scales)—I use the terms concave and convex throughout the book to describe how to weave through the scales. The concave side of a scale is the slightly cupped side of the scale (like a shallow spoon). The convex side of the scale is the slightly domed side.

Stretches
and exercises

You might find yourself with pliers in your hands for several hours a day, which can create undue wear and tear on your hands, wrists, and arms. Chances are you also do most of the ring twisting from your wrists instead of your upper arms.

These stretches and exercises are techniques that I use regularly to keep my wrists and arms in working order. One exercise I do every day is wrist circles. To get started, gently grip your left wrist with your right hand so that your forefinger and middle finger are resting on your arm, and your ring finger and pinkie are resting on your hand. Make a loose fist with your left hand, and slowly rotate your fist clockwise. You may feel lots of little pops and cracks. Not to worry—this just means that you've been working with your hands! Count to 10, and then rotate your hand counterclockwise for another 10 counts. Repeat these steps with your right hand.

I can't stress enough how important it is to stretch—at least your hands and forearms. Making chain mail involves a lot of bending your wrists forward, and a good stretch backwards will nicely counterbalance all of that forward motion. Stretch your left arm out in front of you, hand and fingers pointing up. With your right hand, push the palm of your left hand toward you. Make sure you don't push on your fingers because you can overstretch the muscles in your wrist and forearm. Hold this stretch for 10 seconds. Repeat this process with your right hand.

Prevention is your best weapon against repetitive stress injuries. When you're working at a desk, try to pivot from your lower back to get closer to your workspace instead of slouching with your upper back and shoulders. You can avoid the "double crunch" problem—slouching while working and then keeping your elbows bent all the time—if you follow some simple self-care measures while working. Start good habits early.

Double (or Triple)

When you're asked to double a ring, it means to add a new ring through the exact same path as the previous ring. This means weaving through all of the rings and shapes as the previous ring, as well as weaving in the same direction. Some projects will ask you to complete three times, or "triple."

Scales

Monkey Bells Bracelet

Animal bells add an extra bit of
jingle-jangle sound to this simple
scales bracelet. With just a few rings,
you can create this fun bracelet that
everyone will want to play with. Match
scale colors with other animal shapes
for a wide variety of options.

Supplies

- **25** 16-gauge ¼" ID bronze rings (large)
- **9** 18-gauge ³⁄₁₆" ID bronze rings (medium)
- **4** 18-gauge ⅛" ID copper rings (small)
- **45** ⅞x½" bronze scales
- **5** monkey bells
- Copper-plated toggle clasp
- **2** pairs of flatnose pliers

Before You Begin

- Open all of the rings
- Weave a medium open ring through each of the bells and close; set the bells aside

1. Weave a small open ring through the loop half of the toggle clasp, and close the ring.

2. Weave a medium open ring through the small ring, and close the ring. Double this ring.

3. Weave a large open ring through the convex side of one small scale and the concave side of another. Weave through the two medium rings added in the previous step, and close the ring. Part the two scales.

4. With a large open ring, weave through the convex side of one small scale and the concave side of another. Weave through the large ring from step 3 in between the two previous scales, and close the ring. Part the two new scales.

5. Weave a large open ring through the convex side of a small scale and a medium ring attached to a bell. Weave through the large ring added in step 4, and close the ring. Part the scale from the bell to open up a spot for you to weave the next ring.

6. Repeat step 4 four times. Repeat step 5 to add the second bell.

7. Repeat step 6 three times to attach all five of the bells to the bracelet, with four units of two small scales on one ring in between them.

8. Weave a large open ring through the convex side of one scale and the concave side of another. Weave through the last large ring between the scale and the bell, and close the ring. Part the two scales and repeat this step.

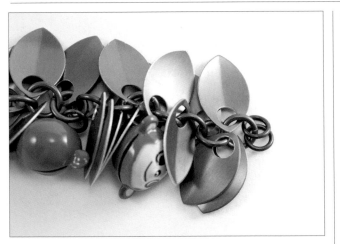

9. Weave a medium ring onto the large ring, in between the last two scales, and close the ring. Double this ring.

10. Create a 1-in-1 chain with small rings to connect the doubled medium rings to the bar half of the clasp (see p. 12).

Four Leaf Clover Bracelet and Earrings

Carry some luck with you wherever you go with fun aluminum shamrocks. This tactile bracelet is surprisingly easy to weave. Little clovers come together in just a few simple steps, and you can connect as many as you need for the length of your bracelet.

Stacked Scale Necklace

Simple yet elegant, this necklace plays with scales and large rings to make a piece that is both substantial and airy. The stacked scales allow you to experiment with pops of color to create a necklace as bold or subtle as you'd like.

Supplies

- **9** 12-gauge ½" ID bright aluminum rings (large)
- **27** 16-gauge ¼" ID bright aluminum rings (medium)
- **4** 10-gauge ~~...~~ ID bright aluminum rings (small)
- **3** 1½x⅞" silver scales
- **2** 1½x⅞" purple scales
- **5** ⅞x½" magenta scales
- Lobster claw clasp
- **9"** bright aluminum cable chain with 19-gauge ³⁄₃₂x⅛" links
- **2** pairs of flatnose pliers
- Wire cutters

Before You Begin

- Close 17 medium rings
- Open all of the remaining rings
- Cut the length of chain in half

1. Weave a medium open ring through the convex side of a small scale and a large scale, and close the ring. Double this ring. Repeat this step with all the scales, creating five stacks of one small scale on top of a large scale in purple or silver.

2. With a large open ring, pick up two medium closed rings. Weave the large ring through the two medium rings attached to a set of magenta and silver stacked scales, and close the ring.

3. With a large open ring, pick up two medium closed rings. Weave this large ring through the medium rings you picked up in the previous step, and close the ring.

4. With a large open ring, pick up two new closed rings and weave through the medium rings attached to a stack of small and purple scales. Weave through the hanging rings from the previous step before closing.

5. Repeat steps 3 and 4 twice. When you first repeat step 3, weave the large ring through the rings attached to the stack of magenta and silver large scales. The second time you repeat step 3, weave the large ring through the stack of purple and magenta scales. As you're adding these stacks of scales, make sure that the convex sides of all the scales are facing you.

6. With the last large open ring, weave through the medium rings attached to a stack of magenta and silver rings, and then the medium rings hanging from a large ring. Close the ring.

7. Weave a small open ring through one end of one of the pieces of chain and a large ring at one end of the focal. Close the ring.

8. With a small open ring, weave through a medium closed ring and the chain at the other end. Close the ring.

9. Repeat step 7 on the other end of the necklace. Weave a small open ring through a lobster claw clasp and the opposite end of the chain. Close the ring.

Chandelier Earrings

Bright aluminum scales fall gracefully from slim aluminum cable chains like fluttering silver feathers. These elegant earrings are perfect for a night on the town, and they're so lightweight that you'll barely notice you're wearing earrings at all.

Supplies

- **38** 18-gauge ⁵⁄₃₂" ID bright aluminum rings (large)
- **18** 18-gauge ⅛" ID bright aluminum rings (small)
- **16** ⅞x½" bright aluminum/silver scales
- 30" aluminum cable chain with 19-gauge ³⁄₃₂x⅛" links
- Pair of surgical steel earring wires
- **2** pairs of flatnose pliers
- Wire cutters

Before You Begin

- For each earring, cut 2 pieces of chain in the following lengths: 1 link, 4 links, 7 links, 11 links
- Close 8 large rings, and open 10 large rings
- Open all of the small rings

1. Weave a small open ring through a scale and an end link of a chain, and close the ring. Repeat to attach a single scale to one end of each chain. Set these aside for now.

2. Weave a large open ring (new rings are shown in green) through four large closed rings, and close the ring.

3. Split the first four rings into two sets of two. With a large open ring, pick up two large closed rings, and weave through one set of two rings. Close the ring.

4. With a large open ring, pick up two large closed rings and weave through the two rings added in the previous step. Close the ring.

5. You now have a chain with four sets of two rings. Attach the ends of this chain to form a square: Weave a large open ring away from you through the front of the two rings on the right side of the chain and back toward you through the back of the two rings on the left side of the chain. Close the ring.

6. Hold the square in your hand so the holes of the stacked sets of two rings are facing you. Weave a large open ring down through the top ring on one of the stacks, and then weave up through the top ring on the stack to the immediate left. Close the ring.

7. Rotate the piece so you're working with the two remaining stacks of rings. Weave a large open ring away from you through the top ring in the right-hand stack and toward you through the back of the top ring on the left-hand stack. Close the ring.

8. Weave a small open ring straight through the two large rings you added in steps 6 and 7. Slip an earring wire onto the ring, and close the ring.

9. Dangle the piece from the earring wire to see the four rings hanging lowest on the piece. You will be using new open rings to attach the chains to these hanging rings.

10. Pinch the end of the earring so the hanging rings are now facing up and out. You should see the front of two of those hanging rings.

11. Weave a large open ring through the chain with seven links and the chain with 11 links. Weave toward you through the back of the ring on the right and away from you through the front of the ring on the left. Close the ring.

12. Rotate the piece counterclockwise 90 degrees. Weave a large open ring through the chain with one link and the chain with four links. Weave toward you through the right-hand ring and away from you through the left-hand ring in the piece. Close the ring.

13. Rotate the piece toward you 90 degrees, and repeat step 11.

14. Rotate the piece toward you 90 degrees, and repeat step 12.

15. Make a second earring.

Tri-Color Jens Pind Necklace

Master this challenging rope weave by working with three colors. Finish it off with large aluminum scales and heart shapes for a textured burst of color. The front closure of this necklace is elegant and seamless.

Supplies

- **5** 14-gauge ³⁄₈" ID bright aluminum/silver rings (large)
- **70** 16-gauge ³⁄₁₆" ID pink rings (medium)
- **70** 16-gauge ³⁄₁₆" ID red rings (medium)
- **70** 16-gauge ³⁄₁₆" ID bright aluminum/silver rings (medium)
- **3** 18-gauge ⁵⁄₃₂" ID bright aluminum/silver rings (small)
- **3** 1½x⅞" pink scales (large)
- **2** 1½x⅞" red scales (large)
- **1½x⅞"** bright aluminum/silver scale (large)
- **2** ⅞x½" bright aluminum/silver scales (small)
- **⅞x½"** pink scale (small)
- **⅞x½"** red scale (small)
- **2** slim bright aluminum/silver hearts
- **2** puffy bright aluminum/silver hearts
- Rhodium-plated toggle clasp
- **2** pairs of flatnose pliers
- EuroPower hole punch pliers

Before You Begin

- Punch a ⅛" hole in each heart shape
- Open all of the rings

1. With the large open rings, create a shaggy shapes chain five units long (see p. 12). Mix up the large and small scales with the hearts as you like. Before closing the last ring, weave it through the loop half of the toggle (not the loop attached to the clasp).

2. Weave a small open ring through the loop of the toggle clasp, and close the ring.

3. Weave a medium open red ring away from you through the front of the small ring, and close the ring.

4. Rotate the red ring away from you. You will see a sideways "eye" shape between the silver and red rings. Weave a medium open pink ring through this eye space, and close the ring.

5. Rotate the pink ring away from you. Weave a medium open silver ring away from you through the red and pink rings, and close the ring.

6. Rotate the weave away from you again. Weave a medium open red ring away from you through the silver and pink rings, and close the ring. Make sure that the left side of this new red ring sits underneath the right side of the red ring before it.

7. Rotate the weave away from you. Weave a medium open pink ring through the red and silver rings, and close the ring. Be sure the left side of the pink ring you're adding sits on top of the right side of the pink ring before it.

8. Rotate the weave away from you. Weave a medium open silver ring through the red and pink rings, and close the ring. Be sure the left side of the new silver ring sits underneath the right side of the first silver ring. The weave is now locked in place with three planes of stacked rings.

9. Rotate the weave away from you. Weave a medium open red ring through the silver and pink rings, and close the ring. Make sure that the left side of the new red ring sits on top of the red ring before it. As you continue rotating, notice the planes of stacked rings.

10. Rotate the piece away from you. Weave a medium open pink ring through the red and silver ring, and close the ring. Be sure the left side of the new pink ring sits underneath the right side of the pink ring before it.

11. Rotate the piece away from you. Weave a medium open silver ring through the pink and red rings, and close the ring. Be sure the left side of the silver ring sits on top of the right side of the silver ring before it.

12. Continue rotating and weaving medium open rings through the piece. When you're weaving a new ring, pay close attention to the rings in the same color before it. The ring you add should be stacked in the same way as the rings before it of the same color. If the rings are stacked like forward slashes, the left side of the new ring sits under the right side of the same color ring before it. If the rings are stacked like backward slashes, the left side of the new ring sits on top of the right side of the same color ring before it.

13. Once you've added all of the medium open rings, weave a small open ring through the last silver and pink rings, and close the ring. Weave another small ring to connect the first small ring to the bar half of the clasp, and close the ring.

Chevron Necklace

With this piece, you'll use three different colors of scales and rings to make a single strip of scale mail. The result is an elegant necklace with clean lines. After you've mastered the technique, use a solid color for an even more dramatic statement.

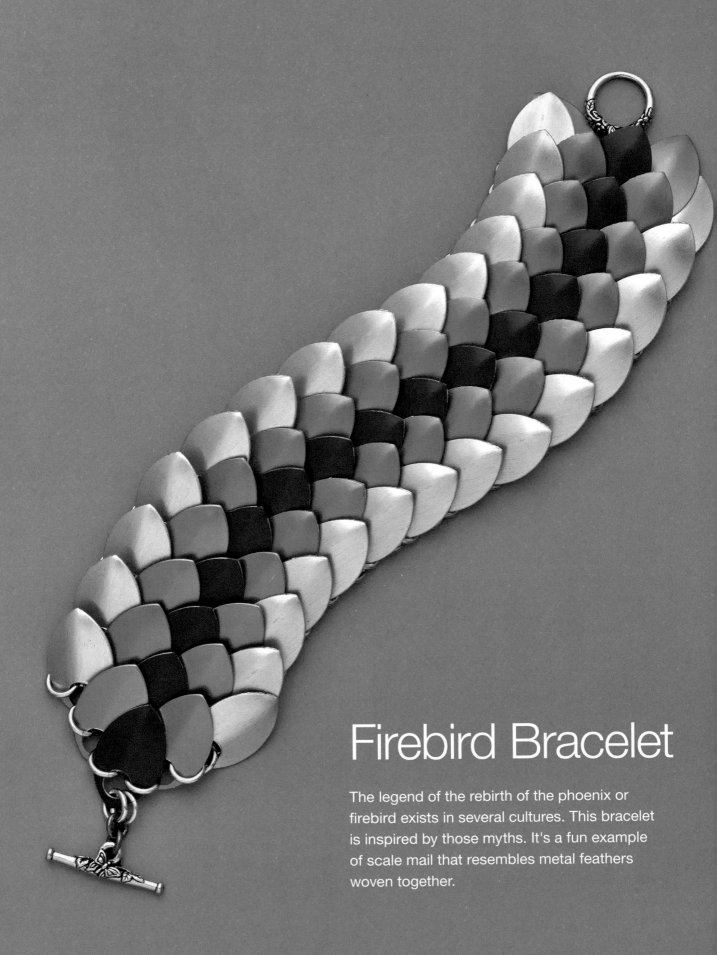

Firebird Bracelet

The legend of the rebirth of the phoenix or firebird exists in several cultures. This bracelet is inspired by those myths. It's a fun example of scale mail that resembles metal feathers woven together.

Supplies

- **26** 18-gauge ¼" ID gold rings (large)
- **160** 18-gauge ³⁄₁₆" ID gold rings (medium)
- **3** 18-gauge ⅛" ID jewelry brass rings (small)
- **15** ⅞ x½" red scales
- **30** ⅞ x½" orange scales
- **28** ⅞ x½" gold scales
- Gold-plated toggle clasp
- 2 pairs of flatnose pliers

Before You Begin

- Open all of the rings

1. Weave a medium open ring through the concave side of an orange scale and the convex side of a gold scale. Close the ring.

2. Orient the scales so that the gold scale is to the left of the orange scale. Weave a medium open ring through the convex side of a red scale and the concave side of the orange scale. Close the ring.

3. Arrange the scales so they form a V shape with the orange scale in the center. Make sure the concave side of each scale is facing you, and make sure the orange scale is stacked in front of and slightly below the gold and red scales.

4. Weave a medium open ring through the concave side of an orange scale, and then weave toward you through the convex side of a red scale. Close the ring. Arrange the orange scale so it sits behind and in between the gold and the red scales.

5. Weave a medium open ring through the convex side of the orange scale and through the concave side of the gold scale. You now have a diamond shape made of scales.

6. Weave a medium open ring through the convex side of a new orange scale, and weave away from you through the concave side of the red scale. Arrange the scale so that it sits in front of and slightly below the red scale.

7. Weave a medium open ring through the convex side of a new gold scale and toward you through the concave side of the orange scale added in step 6. Close the ring. Position the gold scale behind the orange scale. You should see a new V shape on the right-hand side of the piece.

8. Weave a medium open ring through the convex side of a new orange scale and away from you through the concave side of the red scale. Close the ring.

9. Weave a medium open ring through the convex side of the rightmost gold scale and away from you through the concave side of the rightmost orange scale. Close the ring.

10. Weave a medium open ring through the convex side of a new gold scale and away from you through the concave side of the rightmost orange scale. Close the ring. Align the scale so it sits behind the orange scale.

11. Weave a medium open ring through the convex side of a new red scale and away from you through the concave side of the rightmost orange scale. Close the ring. Position the new red scale behind and in between the two orange scales.

12. To connect the red scale securely to the piece, weave a medium open ring through the convex side of the red scale and away from you through the concave side of the leftmost orange scale. Close the ring.

13. Weave a medium open ring through the convex side of a new gold scale and away from you through the concave side of the leftmost orange scale. Close the ring. Position the scale so that it sits behind the orange scale it's attached to and the concave side is facing you.

14. Weave a medium open ring through the convex side of a new orange scale and away from you through the concave side of the rightmost gold scale. Close the ring. Position the orange scale so it sits behind the V shape created by the rightmost gold scale and the center red scale.

15. Weave a medium open ring through the convex side of the orange scale you added in the previous step and away from you through the concave side of the red scale. Close the ring.

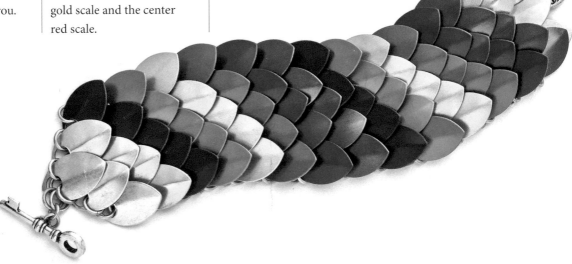

16. Weave a medium open ring through the convex side of a new orange scale and away from you through the concave side of the center red scale. Close the ring. Position the orange scale so it sits behind the V shape created by the center red scale and the leftmost gold scale.

17. Weave a medium open ring through the convex side of the orange scale you added in the previous step and away from you through the concave side of the leftmost gold scale. Close the ring.

18. Repeat steps 10–17 12 more times.

19. Weave a medium open ring through the convex side of a new red scale and through the concave side of the rightmost orange ring. Close the ring. Position the scale so it sits in between and behind the two orange scales.

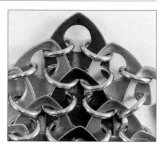

20. Weave a medium open ring through the convex side of the red scale you added in the previous step and through the concave side of the leftmost orange scale. Close the ring.

21. Weave two medium open rings through the red scale. Close the rings.

22. Weave a 1-in-1 chain of two small rings from the pair of medium rings you just added to the bar half of a toggle clasp (see p. 12). This marks the end of the bracelet.

23. Return to the beginning of the bracelet. You will be weaving large rings in between the gold scales through the medium rings. With a large open ring (shown in blue), weave straight up through the back of the second and third medium rings from the bottom on the right side of the bracelet. Close the ring.

24. Weave a large open ring up through the fourth and the fifth medium rings. Close the ring. Repeat this step with each of the next two rings (sixth and seventh, eighth and ninth, etc.) on the right edge of the bracelet.

25. Repeat steps 23 and 24 on the left side of the bracelet.

● **NOTE:** If you like the ruffled edges of the bracelet, you can skip ahead to step 30 to add the second half of the clasp. However, if you prefer a more ordered edge to the bracelet, steps 23–29 will lock the edges in place.

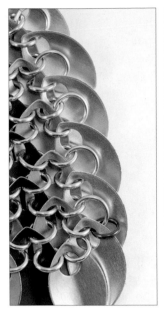

26. Next, anchor the scales to the large rings: Weave an open medium ring through the concave side of the first scale on the bottom edge of the bracelet and through the ring immediately behind it. Close the ring.

27. Weave an open medium ring through the first large ring at the bottom of the bracelet and the concave side of the scale immediately behind it. Close the ring.

28. Repeat steps 26 and 27 along the right edge of the bracelet, using medium rings to attach scales to large rings and large rings to scales.

29. Repeat steps 27 and 28 along the left edge of the bracelet.

30. Return to the beginning of the bracelet. Weave an open medium ring through the medium rings attached to the red scale, and close the ring.

31. Use a small open ring to connect the loop half of the clasp to the medium ring added in the previous step.

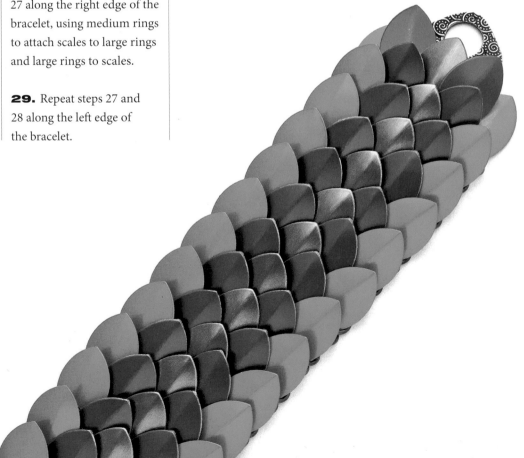

Goddess of the Sun Collar

The goddess Amaterasu is the Japanese goddess of not only the sun, but also the universe. This dramatic necklace was inspired by the myths of her radiance. To make the piece, you'll link together over 500 rings and nearly 200 scales—it's definitely not for the faint of heart! But the result is a beautiful golden necklace fit for anyone who wants to feel divine.

Supplies

- **502** 18-gauge ³⁄₁₆" gold rings (large)
- **4** 18-gauge ⅛" brass metal rings (small)
- **9** 1½x⅞" gold scales (large)
- **194** ⅞x½" gold scales (small)
- Gold-plated toggle clasp
- **2** pairs of flatnose pliers

Before You Begin

- Open all of the brass rings
- Close 136 gold rings and open the rest

1. Weave a small open ring through the loop half of the toggle clasp, and close the ring.

2. Using large rings, create a ribbon of European 4-in-1 that's 34 units long (see p. 12). Make sure the first unit also connects to the small ring attached to the loop of the toggle clasp. Set this ribbon aside.

3. Weave a 1-in-1 chain of three small rings from the bar half of the clasp (see p. 12).

4. Use large rings for the rest of the project. First, create a second ribbon of European 4-in-1 that's 34 units long. Make sure the first unit connects to the last ring in the 1-in-1 chain on the bar half of the clasp.

5a. Flip the ribbons over so the center rings sit under the fanned-out rings on either side. Align the fanned rings on the ends of either ribbon together so one ribbon attached to the loop half of the clasp extends to the right, and the ribbon attached to the bar half of the clasp extends to the left.

b. With an open ring (new rings are shown in blue), weave away from you through the front of the bottom ring on the right ribbon, toward you through the back of the bottom ring on the left ribbon, down away from you through the front of the top ring on the right ribbon, and toward you through the back of the top ring on the right ribbon. Close the ring. Set this ribbon aside for now.

6. Start working with the scales: Weave an open ring through the concave side of one small scale and the convex side of another small scale, and close the ring.

7. Orient the scales so that the concave sides of both scales are facing you and are lying side by side. Weave an open ring through the concave side of a small scale and toward you through the convex side of the scale on the right. Close the ring.

8. Arrange these three small scales into a V shape, with the center scale sitting slightly in front of and below the two outer scales. With an open ring, weave away from you through the concave side of a new small scale and back toward you through the convex side of the right-hand scale. Close the ring.

9. Flip the scale so it sits in the middle of and behind the V shape created by the other scales. Weave an open ring toward you through the back of the convex side of the flipped small scale and the leftmost scale on the original V. Close the ring. You've created a diamond of scales.

10. Weave an open ring (shown in blue) through the concave side of a new small scale and the convex side of the rightmost scale on the diamond. Close the ring.

11. Weave an open ring (shown in blue) through the concave side of a new small scale. Weave through the convex side of the scale you added in the previous step, and close the ring.

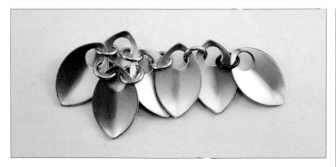

12. Repeat step 11.

13. Swing the scale you added in step 12 around so it sits behind the V created by the three scales before it. Weave an open ring (shown in blue) toward you through the convex side of this scale and then away from you through the right-most scale on the first diamond you created. Close the ring.

14. Repeat steps 10–13 23 times. You will have a line of scale mail diamonds with 25 top points.

15. Flip the line of scale mail over so the convex side of the scales is facing you. You will be attaching these scales to the European 4-in-1 ribbon. Make sure that the ribbon lies flat so there is no twist in the collar. Find the middle scale and the center of the two ribbons. The center ring of the joined ribbons is attached to four rings. Twist the bottom left of these rings open, and slide on the middle scale. Re-close the ring.

16. Repeat step 15 with the bottom right ring. You have now anchored the line of scales to the ribbons.

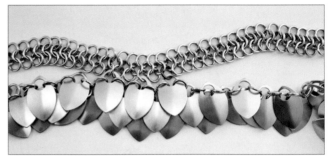

17. Continue attaching scales to the right side of the ribbon: Twist the third ring from the center open (shown in blue), and slide on the next top scale. Re-close the ring.

18. Twist the fifth ring from the center open (shown in blue), and slide on the next top scale. Re-close the ring.

19. Continue re-opening rings and connecting scales. To make the most comfortable necklace, re-open the following rings and add scales to them: 8, 11, 14, 17, 20, 23, 25, 28, 31, and 34 (the number indicates how far from the center ring is).

20. Repeat steps 17–19 to connect the left side of the line of scales to the left side of the European 4-in-1 ribbon.

● **NOTE:**
Stop after step 20 for an understated necklace. Continue on for a more dramatic, embellished version.

21. Next, you will create the scale tendrils. They all start in the same way, and the longer ones simply repeat a few steps more times than the others. Begin by creating the bases for all of them, and then build up the longer tendrils. First, repeat steps 6–13.

22. Weave an open ring through the concave side of a large scale and the concave side of a small scale. Weave up through the convex side of the leftmost bottom scale, and close the ring.

23. Weave an open ring away from you through the right-most bottom scale of the initial piece, and then toward you through the small scale and the large scale you added in step 22. Close the ring.

24. Repeat steps 21–23 six times. Set two of these tendrils aside.

25. Starting with one of the remaining tendrils, weave an open ring (shown in blue) away from you through the concave side of a new small scale and toward you through the convex side of the rightmost top scale. Close the ring.

26. Repeat step 25. Flip this scale toward the center of the of the tendril, between the two points. Weave an open ring (shown in blue) toward you through the convex side of this new scale, and then away from you through the concave side of the leftmost scale on the tendril. Close the ring.

27. Weave an open ring through the concave side of a new small scale, and then weave toward you through the convex side of the top leftmost scale on the tendril. Close the ring.

28. Weave an open ring through the concave side of a new small scale and toward you through the convex side of the top rightmost scale on the tendril. Close the ring.

29. Flip the scale so it sits between the rightmost top scale and the center top scale. Weave an open ring toward you through the scale you flipped and then away from you through the concave side on the center scale of the tendril. Close the ring.

30. Weave an open ring away from you through the concave side of the new small scale and toward you through the convex side of the center scale on the tendril. Flip the scale so it sits between the center and the leftmost scales on the tendril. Weave an open ring toward you through the convex side of the scale you just added, and then away from you through the concave side of the leftmost scale on the tendril. Close the ring, and set this tendril aside.

31. Repeat steps 25–30 on one of the other tendril bases. Repeat steps 25–30 three times on two of the other tendril bases. Repeat steps 25–30 four times to create the longest tendril.

32. Attach the tendrils to the line of scales, starting with the longest tendril: Weave an open ring (shown in blue) away from you through the concave side of the top rightmost scale on the tendril, and then toward you through the convex side of the bottom center scale on the collar. Close the ring.

33. Weave an open ring (shown in blue) away from you through the concave side of the center bottom scale on the collar, and then toward you through the convex side of the leftmost top scale on the tendril. Close the ring.

34. Secure the tendril to the collar by weaving an open ring away from you through the rightmost top scale on the tendril, and then toward you through the next bottom scale on the right side of the collar.

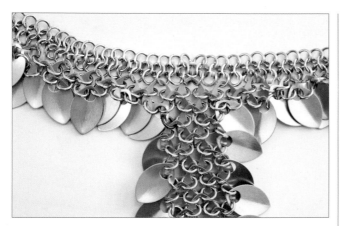

35. Repeat step 33, using an open ring to connect the leftmost scale on the tendril to the next bottom scale on the left side of the collar.

36. Repeat steps 32–35 with one of the second longest tendrils. The "center" scale on the collar you will be attaching the tendril to is the fourth scale from the center.

37. Repeat steps 32–35 with one of the third longest tendrils. The "center" scale on the collar you will be attaching the tendril to is the seventh scale from the center.

38. Repeat steps 32–35 with the shortest tendril. The "center" scale on the collar you'll be attaching the tendril to is the tenth scale from the center.

39. Weave an open ring through the concave side of a large scale and a small scale. Weave toward you through the convex side on the left side of the bottom scale at the end of the necklace, and close the ring. With another open ring, weave away from you through the concave side of the large and small scales, and then up through the convex side of the scale on the collar that's second from the end of the necklace. Close the ring.

40. Repeat steps 36–39 on the left side of the collar.

Disks

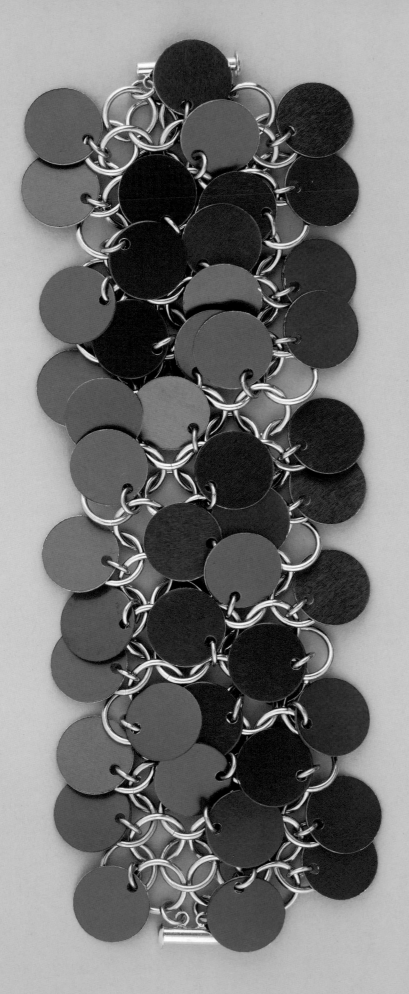

Pretty in Pink Flapper Bracelet

This substantial bracelet jangles with colorful anodized aluminum disks, making it a fun, musical piece. The base is European 4-in-1, which is used to make traditional chain mail armor, while the disks add a 1920s flapper flair.

Supplies

- **53** 18-gauge ⁵⁄₃₂" ID bright aluminum rings (small)
- **108** 16-gauge ³⁄₈" ID bright aluminum rings (large)
- **45** ¹¹⁄₁₆" diameter aluminum disks
- **Silver-plated 4-loop slide clasp**
- **2** pairs of flatnose pliers
- EuroPower hole punch pliers

Before You Begin

- Open all of the small rings
- Open 48 large rings and close the rest
- Punch a ³⁄₃₂" hole near the edge of each disk

1. Weave a small open ring through a loop on the slide clasp. Close the ring. Repeat for each of the four rings on the clasp.

2. Separate the slide clasp. Set one half aside. Using one half, make sure that the "knob" on the end faces left and the small rings point away from you.

3. Using the large rings, create a European 4-in-1 ribbon 15 units long (see p. 12). Make sure that the center ring on the first unit weaves through the small ring on the slide clasp (closest to the knob).

4. Hold the remaining half of the slide clasp, making sure that the knob on this part faces right and the hanging rings point toward you.

5. Return to your strip of European 4-in-1. To finish, weave a large open ring away from you through the front of the right outer ring and toward you through the back of the left outer ring. Weave through the ring opposite the knob on this half of the clasp, and close the ring.

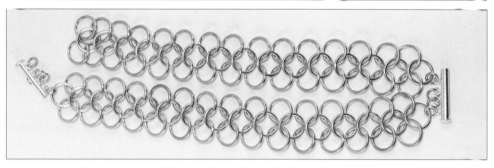

6. Return to the beginning of the bracelet. (The knob faces left and the chain mail strip is on the ring closest to the knob.) On the ring farthest from the knob, repeat step 3 to make a second European 4-in-1 ribbon.

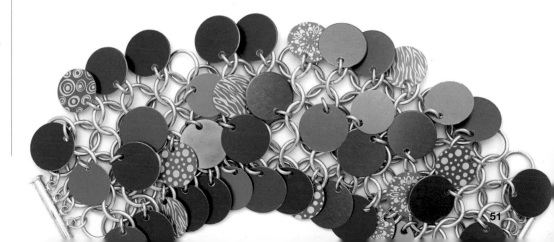

7. Next, attach this strip to the slide clasp: Weave a large open ring away from you through the front right outer ring on the second strip and toward you through the back of the left outer ring. Weave through the rightmost ring on the other end of the slide clasp (closest to the knob), and close the ring.

8. Next, seam up the two strips of European 4-in-1: Weave a large open ring away from you through the front of the first outer ring on the left side of the right strip, through the two remaining rings on the clasp, and up through the back of the first outer ring on the right side of the left strip. Close the ring.

9. Weave a large open ring down through the second and the first outer rings on the left side of the right strip, and then weave up through the first and second outer rings on the right side of the left strip. Close the ring.

10. Continue using large open rings to seam up the two strips of European 4-in-1. Follow the same pattern in step 9, weaving away from you through two rings and then toward you through two rings, lining up the outer rings from the strips.

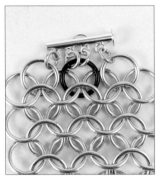

11. After seaming up the strips, finish off the European 4-in-1 base: Weave a large open ring away from you through the last outer left ring on the right strip, toward you through the last outer right ring on the left strip, and through the two remaining rings on the clasp. Close the ring.

12. Remember the "top curve" of the center rings of the European 4-in-1 ribbons? Return to the beginning of the bracelet and find the first top curve. With a small open ring, scoop up a medium disk and weave through this top curve. Close the ring. (You can identify the correct rings by counting the columns of rings from the edge. The disks will be attached to the rings in the even-numbered columns.)

13. Find the next top curve in the column of European 4-in-1. Scoop up a new disk on a small open ring, and weave through this curve. Close the ring.

14. Repeat step 13 until you've attached all the disks to the bracelet.

Maharani Earrings

These earrings have all the bold style and bright colors of an Indian queen's gold and jewels, but none of the weight. Gold, orange, and pink shapes blend together to produce a statement pair of earrings. Little disks dangle from box weave to give the piece a lacy structure.

Butterfly Pin

This sculptural pin uses a tight box chain to form the body of a butterfly. Disks and scales serve as colorful wings, and wire accents finish the piece. You don't need many materials to make this pin, so it's perfect for using up your spare rings and shapes.

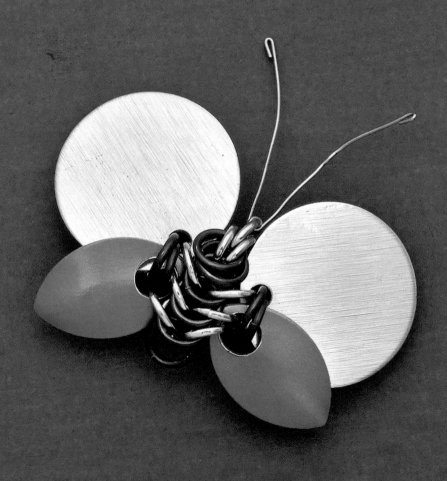

Supplies

- **25** 18-gauge ³/₁₆" ID bronze rings
- **25** 18-gauge ³/₁₆" ID gold rings
- **2** 1" diameter disks
- **2** ⁷/₈x½" scales
- 1" pin back
- 6" 22-gauge enameled copper wire
- 2-part epoxy
- **2** pairs of flatnose pliers
- EuroPower hole punch pliers
- Wire cutters
- Chainnose pliers (optional)

Before You Begin

- Open 2 bronze rings and close the rest
- Open all of the gold rings
- Punch a ⅛" hole near the edge of each disk

1. Weave an open bronze ring through the convex side of a scale and the hole on a disk. Close the ring. Double the ring. Repeat to make the second wing. Set both wings aside.

2. Pick up four closed bronze rings with one open gold ring. Close the ring. Double the ring. Split the set of four bronze rings into two sets of two.

3. Pick up the chain of gold and bronze rings. Let one set of bronze rings on the end fall on either side of the gold set of rings. Pinch these so the gold set of rings parts into a V shape. You should see two bronze rings between the V. With an open gold ring, pick up two closed bronze rings. Weave this open gold ring though the two bronze rings between the gold V, and close the ring. Double the ring.

4. Repeat step 3 twice. Let the last two bronze rings fall down to create a V with the gold rings. Weave an open gold ring through the two bronze rings between the gold rings, and close the ring.

5. Attach the wings to the body: Re-open the gold ring on the bottom left of the body. Slip the orange scale onto the ring, and close the ring.

6. Re-open the gold ring that's second from the bottom on the left side of the body. Slip the orange scale onto the ring, and close the ring.

7. Re-open the third gold ring on the left side of the body. Slip the gold disk onto the ring, and close the ring.

8. Repeat steps 5–7 on the right side.

9. Weave an open bronze ring through the gold V and single gold ring at the top of the butterfly's body, and close the ring to stiffen the top of the body.

10. Bend a 6" piece of wire in half. Thread the wire through the top gold ring on the butterfly's body, and let the ring nest in the bend. Tightly wrap the wire around the gold ring twice to create the antenna. To ensure a tight wrap, squeeze this coil with chainnose pliers.

11. Trim both antennae to about 1½" with wire cutters. Using flatnose or chainnose pliers, bend the last ⅛" of the wire back against itself.

12. Flip the butterfly over, and glue the pin back to the back of the butterfly. Let dry.

● **NOTE:**
For more dynamic wings, punch different sized circles into the disks before assembling.

Rainbow Connection Necklace

Lots of little disks shimmer on this beautiful rainbow necklace. Large aluminum disks serve to anchor the strands of color, while also looking like little puffy clouds.

Supplies

- 25 18-gauge ³⁄₁₆" ID red rings
- 29 18-gauge ³⁄₁₆" ID orange rings
- 35 18-gauge ³⁄₁₆" ID gold rings
- 41 18-gauge ³⁄₁₆" ID green rings
- 45 18-gauge ³⁄₁₆" ID blue rings
- 52 18-gauge ³⁄₁₆" ID purple rings
- 24 16-gauge ¼" ID white rings (large)
- 59 18-gauge ⁵⁄₃₂" ID white rings (small)
- 6 1" diameter matte silver disks

- 50 ³⁄₈" diameter red disks
- 58 ³⁄₈" diameter orange disks
- 70 ³⁄₈" diameter gold disks
- 82 ³⁄₈" diameter green disks
- 90 ³⁄₈" diameter blue disks
- 104 ³⁄₈" diameter purple disks
- Small lobster claw clasp
- 2 pairs of flatnose pliers
- EuroPower hole punch pliers

Before You Begin

- Imagine the 1" disks as a clock's face: On 4 of the disks, punch a ⅛" hole in the positions for 12, 3, 5, 6, and 7; on the 2 other disks, punch a ⅛" hole in the positions for 12, 3, 6, and 9
- Close 44 small white rings
- Open the rest of the rings
- Punch a ³⁄₃₂" hole in each of the ³⁄₈" disks

1. Start with two of the 1" disks with five holes with the same clock position orientation mentioned in "Before You Begin." Flip one of the disks vertically so the three o'clock hole becomes a nine o'clock. Weave a small open white ring through the three o'clock hole on one disk and the nine o'clock hole on the other disk. Close the ring.

2. Position one of the disks with four holes behind the two connected disks. Weave a small open white ring away from you through the front of the three o'clock hole on the left-hand disk, and up toward you through the back of the six o'clock hole on the disk with four holes. Close the ring.

3. Weave a small open white ring away from you through the nine o'clock hole on the right-hand disk, and toward you through the six o'clock hole on the center disk. (You may need to pivot the piece to sneak this ring, is as it's a small space.) Close the ring.

4. To stabilize the piece, weave a small open white ring away from you through the twelve o'clock hole on the left-hand disk, and toward you through the nine o'clock hole on the center disk. Close the ring.

5. To lock the disks into place, weave a small open white ring away from you through the three o'clock hole on the center disk, then toward you through the twelve o'clock hole on the right-hand disk. Close the ring. This completes a cloud cluster.

6. Repeat steps 1–5 with the remaining 1" disks. Set one of the cloud clusters aside.

7. Orient the cloud cluster so the disk with four holes sits in between and behind the other two disks. With an open red ring, pick up two red disks, weave through the five o'clock hole on the large disk on the right, and close the ring. Part the two small disks on the red ring to open up a space. With red rings and red disks, continue creating a shaggy shapes chain until you have 25 red units (50 red disks) hanging from the chain (see p. 12).

8. With an open orange ring, pick up two orange disks and weave through the six o'clock hole on the right-hand disk. Close the ring. With orange rings and orange disks, continue creating a shaggy shapes chain until you have 29 orange units hanging from the chain.

9. Repeat this process of making pieces of shaggy shapes chain with the remaining colors in the remaining holes. The gold chain should be 35 units long, the green chain should be 41 units long, the blue chain should be 45 units long, and the purple chain should be 52 units long.

10. Hold the other cloud cluster, making sure that the disk with four holes is in the center and slightly behind the two other disks. At the end of the red chain, part the two disks. Re-open the last red ring, and weave it through the seven o'clock hole on the left-hand disk in the cluster. Close the ring.

11. At the end of the orange chain, part the two disks. Re-open the orange ring and weave it onto the six o'clock hole on the left-hand disk. Close the ring.

12. Connect the remaining chains in this manner, by re-opening the last link in the chain and weaving it through the next hole on the cloud cluster.

13. Find the top hole in the center disk on one of the cloud clusters. Weave a small open white ring through the hole, and close the ring. Double the ring.

14. With a large open white ring, pick up two small closed white rings, and weave through the previous two small closed rings. Close the ring.

15. Repeat step 14 10 more times. Weave a large open white ring through the last two small rings you added in the chain, and close the ring. With an open small white ring, connect the lobster claw clasp to the large ring.

16. Repeat steps 13–15 on the other cloud cluster, ending with a large white ring instead of a clasp.

Light Up the Night Necklace

Play with color and texture in this necklace. Disks, washers, and rings in black and silver make for an elegant combination, while red and silver offers up some holiday magic.

Supplies

- 14-gauge ⅜" ID bright aluminum/silver ring (extra large)
- **56** 16-gauge ¼" ID red rings (large)
- **32** 16-gauge ¼" ID bright aluminum/silver rings (large)
- **74** 18-gauge ⁷⁄₃₂" ID bright aluminum/silver rings (medium)
- **16** 18-gauge ³⁄₁₆" ID red rings (small)
- **28** 18-gauge ³⁄₁₆" ID bright aluminum/silver rings (small)
- 1½" bright aluminum/silver disk (extra large)
- 1" diameter red disk (large)
- **32** ⅜" diameter red disks (small)
- **48** ⅜" diameter silver disks (small)
- **18** ½" red washers
- 8" bright aluminum cable chain with ⁹⁄₁₆x⅜" 14-gauge links
- 1" silver-plated lobster claw clasp
- **2** pairs of flatnose pliers
- EuroPower hole punch pliers

Before You Begin

- Open all of the rings
- Split the cable chain into 2 equal pieces: Twist the links open and re-close them
- Punch a ⅛" hole near the edge of all of the disks

1. Weave a small open silver ring through the hole in the lobster claw clasp, and close the ring. Double the ring.

2. Weave a small open silver ring through the rings you just added, and close the ring. Double the ring.

3. Twist the link on the end of a piece of chain open, and weave it through the rings you added in step 2.

4. With an open medium ring, pick up two washers, weave through the opposite end of the piece of chain attached to the clasp, and close the ring. Double the ring.

5. Weave an open medium ring through the stack of washers, and close the ring. Double the ring.

6. Weave a five-unit chain of shaggy shapes with small rings and small disks, making sure to attach the first unit to the pair of medium rings you added in step 5 (see p. 12). Alternate the colors so the odd-numbered units are made with small silver rings and disks, and even-numbered units are made with small red rings and disks.

7. Repeat steps 5 and 6 to create another chain of shaggy shapes hanging from the first stack of washers.

8. With a medium open ring, pick up two new washers and weave through the ring of the last unit of one of the shaggy shapes chains, in between the two small disks. Close the ring. Double the ring.

9. Repeat step 8 to connect the second shaggy shapes chain to the new stack of washers.

10. Create Byzantine weave units: Weave a medium open ring through the stack of washers, and close the ring. Double the ring. With a large open silver ring, pick up two large red closed rings, weave through the two medium rings, and close the ring. Double the ring.

11. Let the large red rings fall back toward the medium rings on either side of the large silver rings. Pinch the red rings to part the silver rings and form a V shape. Weave a large open red ring through the two red rings between the silver V, and close the ring. Triple the ring.

12. With a large open red ring, pick up two large closed silver rings, weave through the three red rings from the previous step, and close the ring. Double the ring.

13. Repeat steps 10–12 to create another length of Byzantine chain.

14. Starting with the end of one of the lengths of Byzantine, let the silver rings fall back toward the three red rings, on either side of the two red rings. Pinch the silver rings to part the red rings into a V shape. With an open medium ring, pick up two washers and weave between the silver V through both large silver rings before closing the ring. Double the ring.

15. Working with the second length of Byzantine, let the silver rings fall back and create a V shape. With a medium open ring, weave through the two red rings between the V, and then weave toward you through the back of the washers added in the previous step. Close the ring. Double the ring.

16. Repeat steps 5–15 to complete one side of the necklace. With a medium open ring, weave through the large disk and the extra-large disk, and weave through the stack of washers before closing. Set aside.

17. Weave an extra-large open silver ring through one end of the other piece of chain. Close the ring.

18. On the opposite side of the chain, repeat steps 4–16 with one difference: When you've finished the second set of Byzantine chains, use medium rings to connect those Byzantine chains to the stacked washers at the first end of the necklace.

Fish Scale Earrings

Tiny aluminum disks are woven together with half Persian 3-in-1 to produce a slinky earring that looks like a fish tail. Gold, silver, and a little hint of bronze dance in the light.

Supplies

- **14** 18-gauge ³⁄₁₆" ID silver rings (large)
- **14** 18-gauge ³⁄₁₆" ID gold rings (large)
- **2** 18-gauge ³⁄₁₆" ID bronze rings (large)
- **4** 18-gauge ¹⁄₈" ID silver rings (small)
- **14** ³⁄₈" diameter gold disks
- **14** ³⁄₈" diameter silver disks
- **4** ³⁄₈" diameter bronze disks
- **Pair** of surgical steel earring wires
- **2 pairs** of flatnose pliers
- **EuroPower** hole punch pliers

Before You Begin

- Open all of the rings
- Punch a ³⁄₃₂" hole near the edge of each small disk

1. Weave an open bronze ring through two bronze disks, and close the ring.

2. With an open gold ring, pick up a gold disk. Weave the gold ring through the bronze ring, and close the ring.

3. Rotate the gold ring downward to create a sideways "eye" shape between the two rings. Weave a large open silver ring through this eye, and slip on a silver disk. Close the ring.

4. Pick up a gold disk with an open gold ring, and weave through the silver ring. Close the ring. This new gold ring is stacked above the gold ring before it.

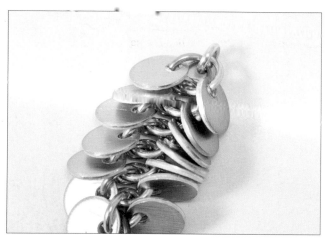

5. Weave a large open silver ring through both gold rings under the silver ring added previously. Slip a silver disk onto the ring, and close the ring.

6. Repeat steps 4 and 5 five more times. Flip the weave over so the disks are facing you. Weave a small open silver ring through the gold and silver rings at the top of the earring, and close the ring.

7. Pick up an earring wire with a small open ring, and weave through the ring added in step 6. Close the ring.

8. Make a second earring.

● **NOTE:**
You can change up the design by attaching the piece to the earring wire so the scales face the back. This reveals the half Persian weave and looks like a slinky spine.

Washers

Washer Barrel Bracelet

This bracelet adds a new twist to barrel weave. Brightly colored anodized aluminum washers replace regular closed rings, adding texture and shape. This dynamic bracelet is surprisingly easy to weave with just a few repeating steps.

Supplies

- **28** 16-gauge ⁵⁄₁₆" ID green rings (large)
- **15** 16-gauge ⁵⁄₁₆" ID gold rings (large)
- **4** 18-gauge ⅛" ID jewelry brass rings (small)
- **28** purple ½" washers
- Gold-plated toggle clasp
- **2** pairs of flatnose pliers
- 3" scrap piece of wire

Before You Begin

- Open all of the rings

1. Weave a small open ring through the loop half of the toggle clasp, and close the ring.

2. With a large open gold ring, scoop up two purple washers, and weave through the small ring attached to the clasp. Close the ring.

3. The two washers are stacked. Slide the top washer on the stack to the right so the washers overlap. Weave a scrap piece of wire through the washers to hold them in place.

4. Weave a large open green ring toward you through the back of the rightmost washer and away from you through the front of the leftmost washer. Close the ring. Remove the wire.

5. Double the ring.

6. With a large open gold ring, scoop up two purple washers and weave straight through the front of both purple washers on the bracelet (don't go through any other rings). Close the ring.

7. Repeat steps 4–6 12 more times. With the last set of washers, repeat steps 4 and 5.

8. Weave a large open gold ring through the last set of washers, and close the ring.

9. Connect the bar half of the clasp to the last gold ring by weaving a 1-in-1 chain of three small open rings to finish the bracelet (see p. 12).

Color Spoke Bracelet

Segments of Byzantine chain connect with anodized aluminum washers to create a colorful, textured bracelet.

Supplies

- **32** 16-gauge ⁵⁄₁₆" ID bright aluminum/silver rings (large)
- **24** 16-gauge ¼" ID purple rings (medium)
- **32** 16-gauge ¼" ID green rings (medium)
- **48** 16-gauge ¼" ID blue rings (medium)
- **2** 18-gauge ³⁄₁₆" ID bright aluminum/silver rings (small)
- **2** 18-gauge ⅛" ID bright aluminum/silver rings (tiny)
- **18** ½" gold washers
- Rhodium-plated toggle clasp
- **2** pairs of flatnose pliers

Before You Begin

- Close all of the green rings
- Open all of the remaining rings

1. With an open purple ring, pick up four closed green rings. Close the ring.

2. Triple the purple ring, and split the four green rings into two sets of two. Repeat steps 1 and 2 to create eight color spokes.

3. Connect the color spokes to stacks of gold washers: With a large open ring, pick up two gold washers and weave through one set of two green rings. Close the ring.

4. Weave a large open ring away from you through the front of the two gold washers added in step 3 and the other set of two green rings attached to the first spoke. Close the ring. The sets of green rings and the washers will form a triangle shape.

5. Flip the triangle over so the stack of washers is facing left. With a large open ring, pick up two gold washers and weave through the bottom stack of green rings. Close the ring.

6. Repeat step 4 with another large open ring. You will now have a diamond shape with stacked gold washers on the longer points.

7. Weave a large open ring through a set of two green rings on a new color spoke and toward you through the back of the two stacked washers. Close the ring.

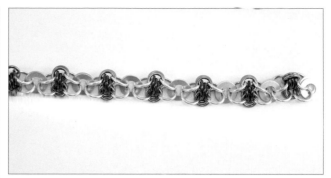

8. Rotate the hanging spoke counterclockwise so the set of green rings on the opposite end of the spoke forms a triangle with the stack of washers and the connected set of green rings. Weave a large open ring away from you through the front of the stacked green rings and then toward you through the back of the washers. Close the ring.

9. Repeat steps 5 and 6 to connect a new stack of washers to the new color spoke.

10. Repeat steps 7–9 to weave all of the spokes and washers together.

11. Pinch one of the color spokes in your hand. Notice how the medium green rings part like lips of an open mouth, exposing the edges of two large silver rings inside them. Weave an open blue ring through these large rings. Close the ring.

12. Triple the blue ring. Repeat steps 11 and 12 on both sides of all color spokes on the bracelet.

13. Weave a small open ring through the ring half of the toggle clasp and the stack of washers on one end of the bracelet. Close the ring.

14. On the opposite end of the bracelet, create a 1-in-1 chain from the washer to the bar half of the clasp. First, attach a small open ring to the washer. Then, attach a tiny open ring to the small ring. Weave a new tiny open ring through the bar and the previous tiny ring.

Washer Cascade Earrings

A simple ribbon of European 4-in-1 serves as the basis for lots of jangling little washers. The cool color fade creates a delicate waterfall of aluminum shapes.

Supplies

- **64** 18-gauge ⁷/₃₂" ID bright aluminum/silver rings
- **12** ½" purple washers
- **12** ½" blue washers
- **8** ½" bright aluminum/silver washers
- Pair of surgical steel earring wires
- **2** pairs of flatnose pliers

Before You Begin

- For each earring, close 10 rings
- Open the rest of the rings

1. Making sure to weave the first ring through the earring wire, weave a European 4-in-1 ribbon five units long (see p. 12). End with a single ring.

2. With an open ring, pick up a purple washer and weave away from you through the front of the bottom ring in the center of the ribbon. Close the ring.

3. With an open ring, pick up a purple washer and weave away from you through the front of the bottom ring on the right side of the ribbon. Close the ring.

4. With an open ring, pick up a purple washer and weave away from you through the front of the bottom ring on the left side of the ribbon. Close the ring.

5. With an open ring, pick up a purple washer and weave away from you through the front of the bottom ring on the right side of the ribbon. Then, weave toward you through the back of the right ring second from the bottom. Close the ring.

6. With an open ring, pick up a new purple washer and weave through the center ring on the ribbon (that is second from the bottom). Close the ring.

7. With an open ring, pick up a purple washer and weave away from you through the front of the bottom ring on the left side of the ribbon, and toward you through the back of the left ring second from the bottom. Close the ring.

8a. Add the blue washers in the same pattern as the purple washers: Weave an open ring with a blue washer away from you through the front of the ring second from the bottom on the right side of the ribbon and back toward you through the back of the ring third from the bottom on the right side. Close the ring.

b. Weave an open ring with a washer through the center ring that's third from the bottom, and close the ring.

c. Lastly, weave an open ring with a washer away from you through the front of the ring second from bottom on the left side and toward you through the back of the ring third from the bottom on the left side. Close the open ring.

9. Repeat step 8 once more, working with the third and fourth rings from the bottom.

10. Repeat step 8, using silver washers instead of blue. Work with the fourth and fifth rings from the bottom.

11. With an open ring, pick up a silver washer and weave through the top ring on the earring. Close the ring.

12. Make a second earring.

Chinese Coin Earrings

I love these little washers because they resemble ancient Chinese coins. This project offers the perfect way to work with washer substitutions in European 4-in-1 chain mail weave.

Supplies

- **20** 18-gauge ³⁄₁₆" ID bright aluminum/silver rings (large)
- **2** 18-gauge ⅛" ID bright aluminum/silver rings (small)
- **10** ½" green washers
- **2** ⁷⁄₁₀" diameter green disks
- Pair of surgical steel earring wires
- **2** pairs of flatnose pliers
- EuroPower hole punch pliers

Before You Begin

- Open all of the rings
- Punch a ³⁄₃₂" hole near the edge of each disk

1. Weave a large open ring through the hole in a disk and through a washer. Close the ring.

2. Weave a large open ring through a new washer and down through the front of the washer attached to the disk. Close the ring. Double the ring.

3. Part the two large rings, and slide the top disk away from you. The two large rings lock in place at a 90-degree angle to the washers.

4. Weave a large open ring through a new washer and down through the front of the washer on the top of the stack. Close the ring. Double the ring.

5. Part the two large rings, and slide the top washer away from you.

6. Repeat steps 4 and 5 until you have woven a stack of five washers together. Weave a large open ring through the top washer in the stack, and close the ring.

7. Weave a small open ring through the large ring you just added and an earring wire. Close the ring.

8. Make a second earring.

Reversible Washer Bracelet

Stacked anodized aluminum washers create a tactile bracelet. This slinky bracelet has an industrial presence with the black side, and a softer feel with the gunmetal side. It's the perfect accessory for any outfit.

Supplies

- **144** 18-gauge ³⁄₁₆" ID bright aluminum/silver rings
- **70** ½" 2-sided black and gunmetal washers
- 4-loop silver-plated slide clasp
- **2** pairs of flatnose pliers

Before You Begin

- Open all of the rings

1. Weave an open ring through the gunmetal side of two washers, and close the ring. Double the ring.

2. Part the two rings so one ring falls to each side of the stack of washers. Slide the top washer away from you to lock the rings in place at the sides of the washers.

3. Weave an open ring through the gunmetal side of a new washer and through the top ring of the stack in the previous step. Close the ring. Double the ring.

4. Split the two rings you just added, and slide the top washer away from you.

5. Repeat steps 3 and 4 32 times to create a ribbon of washers.

6. Flip the ribbon over so the black side of the bracelet is facing you. Orient the piece so the washer closest to you is at the top of the stack. Weave an open ring through the black side of two new washers, up through the back of the first ring on the right side of the piece. Close the ring. Slide the top black washer away from you to make space for the next ring.

7. Weave an open ring away from you through the black side of a new washer and the black side of the top washer you added in the previous step. Then weave up toward you through the back of the second ring on the right side of the left part of the piece. Close the ring.

8. With an open ring, pick up a washer by weaving through the black side. Then weave down away from you through the washer added in step 7 and up toward you through the third closest ring on the left ribbon of washers. Close the ring.

9. Repeat step 8 until you reach the end of the bracelet.

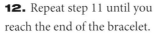

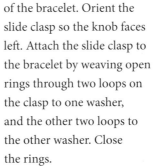

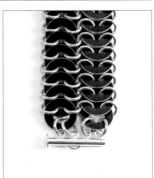

10. Return to the beginning of the bracelet. Weave an open ring up toward you through the back of the first and second washers on the right. Close the ring.

11. Weave an open ring up through the back of the second and third washers on the right, and close the ring.

12. Repeat step 11 until you reach the end of the bracelet.

13. Return to the beginning of the bracelet. Orient the slide clasp so the knob faces left. Attach the slide clasp to the bracelet by weaving open rings through two loops on the clasp to one washer, and the other two loops to the other washer. Close the rings.

14. Repeat step 13 on the opposite end of the bracelet.

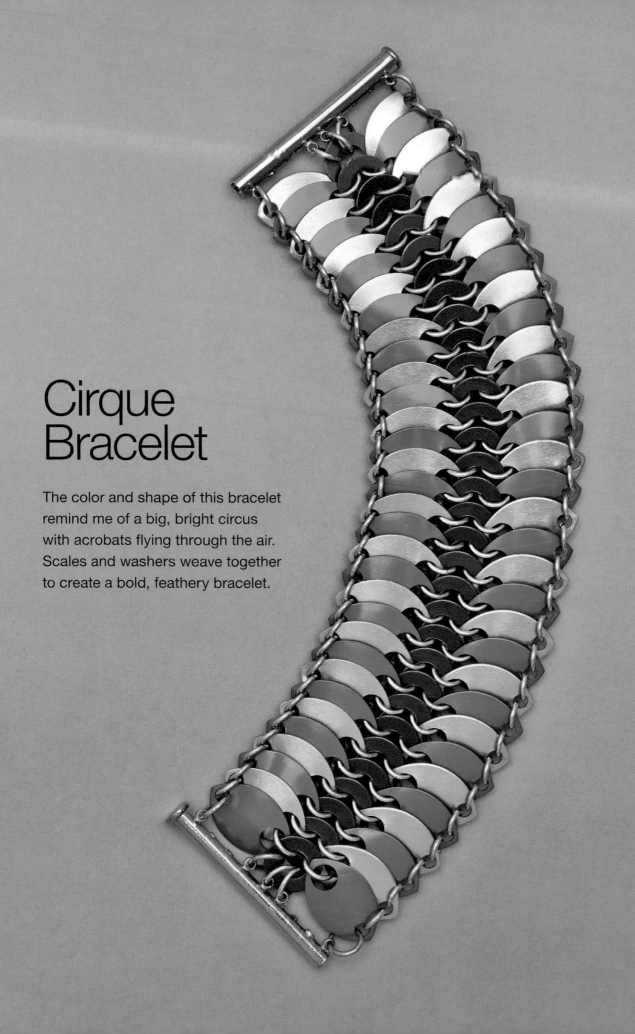

Cirque
Bracelet

The color and shape of this bracelet
remind me of a big, bright circus
with acrobats flying through the air.
Scales and washers weave together
to create a bold, feathery bracelet.

Supplies

- **72** 18-gauge $^7/_{32}$" ID bright aluminum/silver rings (large)
- **62** 18-gauge $^5/_{32}$" ID bright aluminum/silver rings (small)
- **32** $^1/_2$" purple washers
- **32** $^7/_8$x$^1/_2$" gold scales
- **32** $^7/_8$x$^1/_2$" turquoise scales
- 9-loop silver-plated slide clasp
- **2** pairs of flatnose pliers
- EuroPower hole punch pliers

Before You Begin

- Open all of the rings
- Punch a $^1/_8$" hole in the point of each scale opposite the large hole

● **NOTE:**
You are only working with the large holes of the scales in steps 1–6.

1. Weave a large open ring through two washers, the convex side of a turquoise scale, and the convex side of a gold scale. Close the ring. Flip the stacked washers away from you so they're separate from the stack of scales.

2. Weave a large open ring through the concave side of a gold scale and a turquoise scale, and through the stack of two purple washers. Close the ring. Flip this stack of scales away from you so that you have a line of shapes.

3. Weave a large open ring through a new washer and the convex side of a gold scale. Then, weave away from you through the convex side of the turquoise scale on the bottom stack of scales and up toward you through the back of the top washer on the stack. Close the ring. Flip the washer away from you so it sits on the stack.

4. Weave a large open ring through the concave side of a new gold scale, away from you through the top two washers, and then toward you through the back of the turquoise scale on the top stack of shapes. Close the ring. Flip the scale away from you so it sits on the stack of scales.

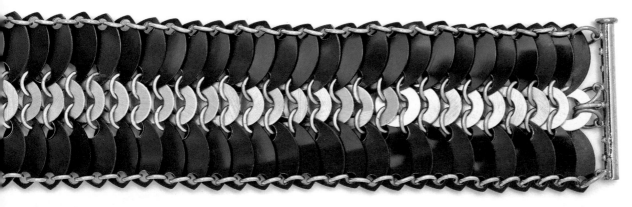

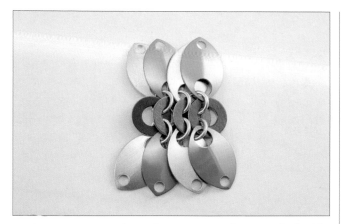

5. Repeat steps 3 and 4 with turquoise scales instead of gold.

6. Repeat steps 3–5 14 times.

7. Return to the beginning of the bracelet. Working with the top edge of the scales, weave a small open ring down through the convex side of a turquoise scale and up toward you through the concave side of a gold scale. Close the ring.

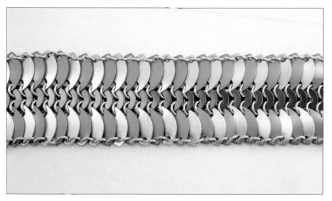

8. Repeat step 7 around the edge of the bracelet, connecting all of the neighboring scales to each other.

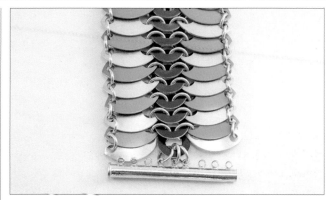

9. Pick up one half of the slide clasp, and make sure the knob is facing left. With open large rings, connect the outer loops of the clasp to the end scales and the middle three loops to the end washer. Close the rings. Repeat this step with the other half of the clasp on the other end of the bracelet.

10. To remove the remaining loops on the clasp, grab the base of the loop with your pliers. Twist your pliers to remove the loop.

Gallery

Aluminum shapes aren't just for making jewelry. My wearable chain mail art pieces have been featured on Broadway, on television, and in juried art shows across the country. Here is a small sample of what else you can do with these wonderful disks, washers, and scales.

Large Leaf Necklace Photo by Pete Feyerherd

Flapper Dress Photo by Megan Sontag, model Oksana May

Breastplate of Apollo
Photo by Larissa Zageris, model Desiree Stypinski

Knight's Wear Photo by Larissa Zageris, model Desiree Stypinski

Phoenix Jacket
Photo by Edwin R. Ruiz, hair/MUA by Genell Banks, asst. camera Ian Short, producer Ladie K Productions, model Ladie K

Wedding Dress
Photo/MUA by Larissa Zageris

Mermaid Armor
Photo by Larissa Zageris, model Desiree Stypinski

Ninja
Photo by Treavor Doherty

Kimono Photo by
Megan Sontag, model Oksana May

Disco Poncho Photo/
MUA by Larissa Zageris, hair by
Michael Hopkins, model Ladie K

Red Lizard Vest Photo/MUA by Larissa Zageris, hair by Michael Hopkins, model Ladie K

Elegant Chain Photo by Pete Feyerherd, model Ladie K

Blue Leaves
Photo by Pete Feyerherd

Acknowledgments

There are so many people I want to thank for their support over the years. First and foremost, I want to give huge thanks to my mom for all of her support. My thanks also go to my aunts Mary, Mary, and Joy, my uncle John (to whom I still owe a commission, for his idea that I write a standards and practices article for their mail) and grandmother. Big thanks to the friends who kept me sane with art and love—especially Mary Lou and Allyson—while I was stressing out. I consider myself tremendously lucky to have so much support.

Big thanks to Ladie K and Larissa Zageris, two of the hardest-working people I know. I have worked with Ladie K since I first got started making jewelry full time, and her modeling and production skills have helped my business in more ways than I can count. Larissa is a brilliant artist who has brought depth and life to my work with her photographs. I am so lucky that these two ladies continue to work with me on projects.

I want to thank everyone at Kalmbach for making this book happen. Most of all, I'd like to thank my editor, Erica Swanson, for believing in me and my vision for the book through all of my health problems. I cannot thank her enough. I'd also like to thank Dianne Wheeler for taking a chance on me, Carole Ross, Bill Zuback, and Jim Forbes for making the book look great, and Linda Franzblau, Jami Rinehart, and Janice Zimdars for their marketing efforts.

Thanks go to Kathy and Rebeca for teaching me how to run a business and showing me that it is possible to make a living creating art if you're smart about it.

Most of all, I'd like to thank my grandfather, Felicjan Walilko. He gave me permission to be free and gave me everything.

About the Author

Vanessa Walilko is a chain mail jewelry and wearable art designer from Chicago, Ill. Her chain mail fashion has been featured in international exhibitions, and her chain mail costumes have appeared in Broadway's *Pippin* and the movie *Night at the Museum 3*. Her jewelry has been shown at juried art fairs around the country, including shows at the Museum of Arts, Houston, and the Indianapolis Museum of Art. Vanessa has been teaching the art of chain mail for more than seven years, showing students throughout the United States and Canada how to link lots of little rings together to make fun, wearable jewelry. When she doesn't have pliers in her hands, she can be found writing and performing around Chicago.

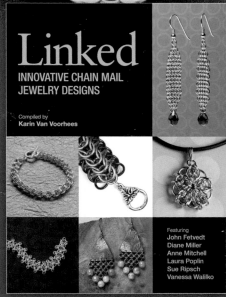

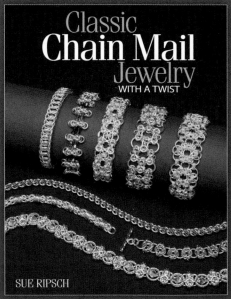